Pandemic Preaching:

Preaching the Gospel in Times of Crisis

A Book By

Bishop Kenneth W. Paramore, D. Min.

Ready Media LLC

Copyright © 2021 by Bishop Kenneth W. Paramore, D. Min.

Publisher: READY Media LLC

Printed in the United States of America

ISBN: 978-1-7358073-2-4

All rights reserved. No part of this book may be used or reproduced by any means, graphic, electronic, or mechanical, including photocopying, recording, taping or by any information storage retrieval system without the written permission of the author except in the case of brief quotations embodied in critical articles and reviews.

Contents

Chapter 1 | Knowing the Crisis   1

Chapter 2 | Knowing the Cause   15

Chapter 3 | Knowing the Times   20

Chapter 4 | Knowing the Effects   28

Chapter 5 | Knowing the Cost   36

Chapter 6 | Knowing the Fears   41

Chapter 7 | Knowing the Demographic   48

Chapter 8 | Knowing the Lord & The Word   68

Chapter 9 | Conclusion   80

Introduction

March 6-8, 2020 was a great weekend for me. Our reformation, Lifted Reformation of Christian Churches was set to consecrate our first Bishop. All roads led to Atlanta and everything was exciting. Soon to be Bishop John S. Battle III was ready. His two churches New Shield of Faith and Spread The Word Christian Ministries were ready. They had done a masterful job navigating their pastor's Episcopal year and all systems were go.

We had a glorious time all weekend long. The facility was packed. The clergy community showed up in overwhelming numbers. The churches were in great attendance and the Lifted staff was impeccable. God moved in a mighty way for us. The weekend was perfect, except for one thing.

We noticed during the consecration on March 8, that one of the officers of the church was being carried out on a gurney. The paramedics had to come and pick him up because he was having trouble with his pacemaker. We simply prayed and trusted God for his healing. As we made our way back to the airport, we noticed a very somber feeling in the air. Almost like that of September 11, 2001 but not quite as looming and ominous.

Word had begun to spread over the news about a virus that was getting out of hand and it was making everyone nervous.

We made it home safely only to find out that the officer who went to emergency room that day ended up contracting the virus known as the Coronavirus and was in critical condition. We were relieved to find out later that he contracted the virus in the hospital and not at the consecration services. However, this would prove to be the beginning of one of the most difficult times we would ever face as citizens of the United States and even occupants of this planet in these current times.

Literally, we missed the pandemic by one week. It appears that the Lord wanted John S. Battle III to be consecrated to the office of Bishop because that very next week things slowly begin to shut down all over the country, and around the world.

In fact, Bishop Battle's father in-law died two weeks after the consecration. Because of my relationship with the family, I immediately went back to Georgia.

My ticket (roundtrip) was only thirty-five dollars and there were only nine people on the flight going and twelve returning. From that place, every week we watched this monster known to us as Covid-19 get more and more out of hand as each day passed.

While our governor, Mike DeWine, is lauded across the country as being a trailblazer in his response to and containment of the virus in the state of Ohio, it has still been an overwhelming experience every step of the way.

It has been nothing less than absolute despair and chaos since our state began to systematically shut down. People have been getting sick and unfortunately dying. Businesses have had to close their doors forever. Families are struggling to make ends meet. Our government is giving us mixed signals. The medical community and its authorities are at odds on what we should do to protect ourselves. The conspiracy theorists are having a field day. While all of this is happening the Church of Jesus Christ is waiting for secular society to tell us whether, or not we are essential. It is altogether a difficult, different, depressing and debilitating time.

The question is what is the response of the prophet to all

this that is going on?

We need something, because it appears that on top of Covid-19 having its way with the community at large, racism and social injustice has reared their ugly heads again in some of the most profound ways. Ahmaud Arbery, George Floyd, and Breonna Taylor all were murdered either by law enforcement or those who believed they were acting in sync with law enforcement and it left the country in intense protest both near and far.

So, with a virus spreading like wildfire, social injustice and demonstrations reaching a boiling point, as well as it being an election year, what is the message that is coming from the pulpit?

I am an advocate of keeping the people at large and the people of God safe. However, something must come from the preachers other than, "stay home and help save lives." The country is seemingly unraveling, and we are okay to just admonish the people to stay home and wait for things to get better?

When Donald Trump became president of our United States, for the first time in my life I was embarrassed to be an American. I could not understand for the life of me how we could put someone in office knowing how much he had transgressed all the ethical lines he did even before he became a presidential candidate. It also pained me even more to be confronted with on a regular basis the lines of decency and diplomacy he has obliterated while in office. I am embarrassed to call him my president.

Now, because of these things I am embarrassed to be called a preacher. With all the hell that we find ourselves navigating, the church and its leadership is alright saying, "stay at home and save lives". Should not there be a more instructive message coming from pulpits across the country?

To add insult to injury I witnessed young and old people

band together and risk their lives to protest the blatant injustices that were happening all to regular. They took to the streets in pandemic across the world. However, in even larger numbers the churches remained padlocked. We refused to even open for a prayer meeting to bring hope back to our communities.

It was at this point that I began to pray and ask God what I could do to help. God gave me this assignment. He told me to put together a class or a book to help preachers and pastors not only respond to this pandemic but prepare for the next time a season of crisis happens.

I reasoned, it could be that we were waiting on society or the medical community to tell us what to do because we had never seen anything like this before. However, we do have our marching orders. We are supposed to preach in season and out of season. That is what Paul tells us in 2 Timothy chapter 4. Well, God has given us a lengthy "in" season over the past 25-30 years in the Body of Christ. We have experienced promotion and affluence in church on a grand scale. It appears that we have finally reached our "out of season" and we are tapping out for fear of what might happen.

The Body of Christ still needs a word and a witness. While Covid-19 is both serious and deadly, we cannot shrug our shoulders at the charge we have as men and women of God. Unfortunately, we don't get to preach an entire lifetime and never be in harm's way. This is our "out of season" and the Lord has need of us. We do not have the threat of crucifixion, or the lion's den, or even being stretched asunder or beheaded and burned in oil. We merely need to wear masks, alter our services and sanitize our facilities and we refuse to do that.

The Church needs a message. The message need not be to satiate itching ears either. We need to lay on our faces and get a word from the Lord for these trying times that we have never seen before. I am convinced that when we find ourselves in times we have never been in before, God will give us a word that we have never heard for His people and ourselves.

That is the purpose of this book. It is our effort to help preachers understand and know what Pandemic Preaching should sound and look like. I would like to share my thoughts and create dialogue about how we should alter attendance and services, yet remain vigilant for the cause of the Kingdom. Yea, even how to research and put together messages that speak to the terror and fear of the masses. This is necessary because when they go through, we also go through. In this season of our "going through" the question becomes how indeed do we engage in a hermeneutic that will conquer a crisis?

This is what we intend to discuss in the next few pages of this work.

Chapter 1
Knowing the Crisis

The Coronavirus is not a new virus. Scientists first identified a human coronavirus in 1965. It caused a common cold. Later that decade, researchers found a group of similar human and animal viruses and named them after their crown-like appearance.

Seven coronaviruses can infect humans. The one that causes SARS emerged in southern China in 2002 and quickly spread to twenty-eight other countries. More than 8,000 people were infected by July 2003, and 774 died. A small outbreak in 2004 involved only four more cases. This coronavirus causes fever, headache, and respiratory problems such as cough and shortness of breath.

MERS started in Saudi Arabia in 2012. Almost all the nearly 2,500 cases have been in people who live in or travel to the Middle East. This coronavirus is less contagious than its SARS cousin but more deadly, killing 858 people. It has the same respiratory symptoms but can also cause kidney failure.

In 2016, a 45-year-old schoolteacher in Athens, Greece, arrived at the emergency room of the Hygeia Hospital. A non-smoker with no major health issues, she presented with unusual symptoms— a fever over 103 degrees, a dry cough and severe headache. When the ER doctor examined her, it was noted that the lower part of her left lung was rattling when she breathed, and a chest X-ray confirmed an abnormality.

Thinking this a case of bacterial pneumonia, doctors treated her with antibiotics. But over the next two days, the woman's condition deteriorated—and the pneumonia lab test came back negative. As her breathing began to fail, she was supplied with oxygen and a new set of medications. Meanwhile, she was tested for a broad variety of possible culprits, including various strains of the flu, the bacteria that cause Legionnaires disease, whooping cough, and other serious respiratory diseases. All came back negative, as did tests for SARS and MERS.

In fact, only one test turned up positive, but it was a result so surprising that doctors ran it again. The result was the same: the patient was suffering from a familiar but inscrutable infection known as 229E—the first human coronavirus ever discovered.

The novel Corona virus outbreak, which began in Wuhan, China, in December 2019, has expanded to touch nearly every corner of the globe. Hundreds of thousands of people around the world have been sickened and thousands of others have died. The World Health Organization has declared the virus a global health emergency and rated COVID-19's global risk of spread and impact as "very high," the most serious designation the organization gives.

Here's a timeline of how the outbreak has unfolded so far:

Dec. 31, 2019: WHO says mysterious pneumonia sickening dozens in China

Health authorities in China confirm that dozens of people in Wuhan, China, are being treated for pneumonia from an unknown source. Many of those sickened had visited a live animal market in Wuhan, but authorities say there is no evidence of the virus spreading from person to person.

Jan. 11, 2020: China reports 1st novel coronavirus death
Chinese state media reports the first death from novel coronavirus, a 61-year-old man who had visited the live animal market in Wuhan.

Jan. 21, 2020: 1st confirmed case in the United States
A man in his 30s from Washington state, who traveled to Wuhan, is diagnosed with novel coronavirus. Japan, South Korea and Thailand also report their first cases one day prior.

Feb. 5, 2020: Diamond Princess cruise ship quarantined
More than 3,600 passengers are quarantined on a cruise ship off the coast of Yokohama, Japan, while passengers and crew undergo health screenings. The number of confirmed cases on board the ship would eventually swell to more than 700, making it one of the largest outbreaks outside of China.

Feb. 11, 2020: Novel coronavirus renamed COVID-19
The WHO announces that novel coronavirus' formal new name is COVID-19. "Co" stands for coronavirus, "Vi" is for virus and "D" is for disease. Health officials purposely avoid naming COVID-19 after a geographical location, animal or group of people, so as not to stigmatize people or places.

Feb. 26, 2020: 1st case of suspected local transmission in United States
The Centers for Disease Control and Prevention (CDC) confirms the first case of COVID-19 in a patient in California with no travel history to an outbreak area nor contact with anyone diagnosed with the virus. It's suspected to be the first

instance of local transmission in the United States. Oregon, Washington and New York soon report their own cases of possible community transmission.

Feb. 29, 2020: 1st death reported in United States
The first COVID-19 death is reported in Washington state, after a man with no travel history to China dies on Feb. 28 at Evergreen Health Medical Center in Kirkland, Washington. Two deaths that occurred Feb. 26 at a nearby nursing home would later be recorded as the first COVID-19 deaths to occur in the United States. Later still, a death in Santa Clara, California, on Feb. 6 would be deemed the country's first COVID-19 fatality after an April autopsy.

March 3, 2020: CDC lifts restrictions for virus testing
The CDC issues new guidance that allows anyone to be tested for the virus without restriction. Previously, only those who had traveled to an outbreak area, who had close contact with people diagnosed with COVID-19, or those with severe symptoms, could get tested.

March 13, 2020: Trump declares national emergency
President Donald Trump declares a U.S. national emergency, which he says will open up $50 billion in federal funding to fight COVID-19.

March 15, 2020: CDC warns against large gatherings
The CDC warns against holding or attending gatherings larger than 50 people, including conferences, festivals, parades, concerts, sporting events and weddings for eight weeks,

recommending that individuals cancel or postpone those events to avoid spreading the virus or introducing it into new communities.

March 17, 2020: Coronavirus now present in all 50 states
West Virginia reports its first COVID-19 case, meaning the disease is present in all 50 states.

March 17, 2020: Northern Californians ordered to 'shelter in place'
Six counties in the San Francisco area ordered to "shelter in place" for three weeks, meaning residents are required to remain at home unless they are leaving the house for an essential reason, or are exercising outdoors.

March 18, 2020: China reports no new local infections
China reports no new domestic infections in the country for the first time since the outbreak began. If the trend holds for 14 days, it could be a sign that China's outbreak is ending. The country is still seeing travel-related COVID-19 cases and it remains to be seen whether China will be able to prevent a second wave of infection, once the government's strict lockdown measures are lifted.

March 19, 2020: Italy's death toll surpasses China's
Italy's death toll tops 4,000, making it the first country to report more overall deaths than China, despite its much smaller population. The following week, COVID-19 deaths in Spain would similarly eclipse deaths in China.

March 20, 2020: New York City declared US outbreak epicenter

New York City state reports that more than 15,000 people have tested positive for COVID-19 and account for roughly half of the infections in the country. The vast majority of New Yorkers with COVID-19 are in the New York City region, which Mayor Bill de Blasio calls "the epicenter of this crisis," warning that the outbreak will get worse as supplies dwindle.

March 24, 2020: Japan postpones Olympics

Japan postpones the 2020 Summer Olympics, which were originally slated to be held in Tokyo starting July 24, until summer 2021. Countries including Canada and Australia had already announced that given the public health risk of the COVID-19 pandemic, they would not be sending their athletes to the Games.

March 24, 2020: India announces 21-day complete lockdown

Indian Prime Minister Narendra Modi announces a total ban on the country's 1.3 billion citizens leaving their homes for 21 days, in order to stop the spread of COVID-19.

March 26, 2020: United States leads the world in COVID-19 cases

The United States now has more confirmed coronavirus cases than any other country in the world, with cases topping 82,000 and deaths topping 1,000.

March 27, 2020: Trump signs $2 trillion stimulus bill

President Donald Trump signs a $2 trillion coronavirus relief bill into law. The law guarantees loans to small businesses and creates a lending system for distressed companies. It also provides financial aid to hospitals on the frontlines of the crisis.

March 27, 2020: UK Prime Minister Boris Johnson tests positive
Boris Johnson, the prime minister of the United Kingdom, tests positive for COVID-19 after having a high fever and persistent cough. Johnson will continue to lead the government via video conferences.

April 2, 2020: Global cases hit 1 million
More than 1 million people around the world have been diagnosed with COVID-19. Given testing shortages, undiagnosed cases and suspicions about governments obscuring the scope of their respective outbreaks, the actual number of people sickened is believed to be much higher.

April 4, 2020: New York sets single-day record for new COVID-19 cases
New York State logs a record 12,000 new COVID-19 cases in a single day.

April 9, 2020: Evidence that first COVID-19 cases in NYC came from Europe
A new study finds evidence that the first COVID-19 cases in New York City originated in Europe and occurred as early as February. Researchers traced the origin of New York City's outbreak and found it was primarily linked to untracked

transmission between the U.S. and Europe, with limited evidence showing direct introductions from China or other countries in Asia.

April 21, 2020: Autopsy revels 1st US COVID-19 death was earlier than previously thought
The CDC confirms that tissue from an individual in Santa County, California, who died Feb. 6 tested positive for COVID-19 . That death occurred weeks earlier than the COVID-19 deaths in the Seattle area on Feb. 26 that were previously believed to be the nation's first.

May 27, 2020: US reaches 100,000 deaths
The pandemic has now killed more than 355,000 people worldwide and more than 100,000 people in the United States.

May 31, 2020: George Floyd's killing spurs mass protests
After video surfaces of a Minneapolis police officer kneeling on a black man's neck for nearly nine minutes, ultimately killing him, protests against police brutality and systemic racism erupt across the country. Public health experts initially worry that the large-scale protests will spark an increase in COVID-19 cases, but the protests are never linked to such a spike.
MORE: Police reformers push for de-escalation training, but the jury is out on its effectiveness

June 11-17, 2020: Cases in Arizona, South Carolina and Florida soar
States that rushed to reopen their economies saw subsequent rises in COVID-19 cases, hospitalizations and deaths.

June 24, 2020: NY, NJ, Conn., require 14-day quarantine for travelers from Florida
As the United States' outbreak shifts from the Northeast to the South and West, several states put restrictions on travelers from Florida.

June 30, 2020: EU says it will reopen borders to 14 countries, but not the US
The European Union announces that it will lift restrictions on travelers from 14 nations. Because of rising coronavirus cases in the United States, the U.S. is not included on the list of approved countries.

July 7, 2020: US submits formal notice that it will withdraw from the WHO
The United States notifies the World Health organization that it is dropping out of the global health collective. The departure will go into effect in July 2021.

July 11, 2020: Trump wears a mask in public for the first time
President Donald Trump wears a mask in public for the first time throughout the pandemic, during a visit to a military hospital.

July 12, 2020: Florida breaks single-day record for new COVID-19 cases
Florida logs 15,000 new COVID-19 cases in a single day, surpassing New York's one-day record of 12,000 in April.

July 26, 2020: Florida surpasses New York in total coronavirus cases
Florida's 423,855 known COVID-19 cases now exceed cases in New York state, the early epicenter of the nation's outbreak.

Please note that this timeline ends in July 2020 due to publishing and printing deadlines. There are more key events to research to give even more clarity to this pandemic and the social injustices that we have been dealing with all year.

What makes this so problematic is the lack of cohesiveness between the powers that be. Each entity that is supposed to be set up to encourage us, protect us and instruct us makes it more difficult to navigate. Somewhere between our political leaders, medical leaders and media outlets we did not know what to do, or what to believe.

Our President, Donald Trump comes out in the wake of this pandemic telling us that everything is alright, and it will be over before we know it. Day after day and week after week our commander in chief continued to lie to us and tell us that in a very short while things would go back to normal and there would be very little fallout from virus.

Even in the wake of so much death Trump's pride would not allow him to even wear a mask until he was made to because he was visiting a hospital. Our leadership has been terrible.

Along with this has been all the confusion that came from medical community on the matter. Wear masks don't wear masks. Wear gloves don't wear gloves. Social distancing, but we are going to open bars. Social distancing but we are going to open beaches. Here are your symptoms, unless you don't have them. Here's how you treat it, there is no treatment. The curve is flattening or is it the fact that we don't have tests available and as soon as we have tests available there will be surges everywhere. It has been one giant ball of confusion.

In all of this, people are looking for direction on what to do and how to handle themselves. Because we are now isolated and unable to move around tension becomes an issue and it should be no surprise that levels of suicide, racism, domestic violence and social injustice begin to climb because people are now being driven by their primal instincts be it good, bad or ugly.

It is not a coincidence that during this time we run into such cases as Ahmaud Arbery, George Floyd, Breonna Taylor, and Rayshard Brooks. It is also not coincidental that we get to the place where protests and riots breakout in response to the lack of justice and order that is being shown in these very simple cases of racism, extreme force and police brutality.

In all of this, my heart became heavy when I started noticing how uninvolved the church was in everything that was going on.

Here in our state of Ohio our governor never really closed the churches. He strongly advised that we not meet. The problem is that when he began to reopen society, he never strongly advised us to return to church. This being the case, people now have a fear of coming to church. They will go to Walmart, restaurants, public parks, beaches and work. But they remain either petrified or indifferent to the notion of returning to church.

The irony in all this is that church is the least frequented place of any on the list of establishments that are open. We can even curtail the use of church further where it is one day a week for one hour. We can then spend the next 6 days sanitizing and cleaning the church for the next service. We can even bring service times down to under an hour. But none of this is being or has been done on any mass level.

In fact, many pastors of Christian churches have decided that they will not gather for worship in their churches until the CDC says it is okay to do so. What is peculiar to me is no one from the CDC has come out publicly and asked the faith community to pray for them so that they can be led by God in their research, findings, and protocols.

It appears that the church has more faith in the secular entity than the CDC has in the church as an entity of faith. For me, the irony in this is thick.

Even in the protests that we have seen it appears that the church has gone silent.

It is my premise that no voice in times like these should be louder than the voice of faith and wisdom. I began to ask myself why are the preachers so quiet? Then it dawned on me, we are so quiet because we do not know what to say.

We have been so long giving canned sermons and prepared responses that in the day of crisis we have seemingly forgotten how to lay before the Lord and get a real word that can help real people through a real crisis.

This is when I began to pray. The prayer was quite simple. It went something like, "Lord, I don't know what to do, or what to say. I am scared and I am scared for my children, my family and for the people I lead. I need you God to please show me what to do. I need you God to please give me what to say. Show me how to glorify you and edify your people in this most impossible moment." That was my prayer.

This is the prayer I have prayed since March 2020 even until now. I pray this prayer without ceasing because I do not know what to do. I pray this prayer because I do not know what is going on. The politicians are not honest. I feel the news to be edited and deceptive. I am afraid that the doctors and scientists are not transparent. I need You God to show me what to do and to give me what to say.

God has been faithful. One week at a time He has been answering prayers and giving direction.

First things first. You cannot preach if there is no place from which to preach.

God instructed me to keep our church open. We have been open every Sunday during the pandemic and God has blessed us richly. Many would like to say that staying open was my idea. It was not. It was what the Lord instructed me to do.

Because of the congregational make up that we have at Christ Centered Church, God told me that we could not close because I had too many people that would return to their pre-salvific existence. Many of them were not strong enough to have church solely on social media or discipline themselves to study or worship away from the local assembly. This they stated by their own admissions. So, we stayed open.

We stayed open for the minority, not for the masses.

I immediately had to put together a team of people who would make sure that our facility was sanitized every week. I also had to encourage my seniors to stay home and not come to church, along with anyone who had compromised immune systems. I also told the people who were frightened about coming to church to stay home and that no one would penalize them or judge them because they were not coming.

Finally, I had to create seating that accommodated the mandates for social distancing. I also had to shorten the worship service and omit altar appeals and prayers until we found our way out of this pandemic. Also, we would make certain that every Sunday Service would be on social media so that the people could worship from home and still feel connected.

All weekly rehearsals, meetings and appointments have been canceled until further notice. This is inclusive of Bible Study and Sunday School. The worship service we do have is once a week for 55 minutes to 1 hour. This is how we have proceeded with corporate worship and so far by the grace of God we have not had any cases of Covid-19 in our churches.

We have stations set up at the entrances that conduct temperature checks and conducts a survey before each service and we have had to send some people home either because of their temperature or they had been in contact with someone who had or has Covid-19.

Please understand, I am not suggesting that every church do what we have done. However, I am suggesting that every pastor do what I did. That is, lay on your face and talk to God the old-fashioned way about what his will and direction is for your church and its people. This must be done in any crisis.

2 Chronicles 20:12
O our God wilt thou not judge them? for we have no might against this great company that cometh against us; neither know we what to do: but our eyes are upon thee.
KJV

The prophet is clear. We are confused and do not know what to do. Therefore, we turn our attention to you. We are looking for you to show us Lord. You and you, alone.

Chapter 2
Knowing the Cause

2 Timothy 4:2
Preach the word; be instant in season, out of season; reprove, rebuke, exhort with all longsuffering and doctrine.
KJV

This is a favorite passage for clerics to use during times of elevation. We love to tell ministers and elders who are being ordained or installed into various offices that this is the requirement of the Lord. We tell them to be instant in season and out of season. We tell them to preach when they feel like it and preach when they don't. We tell them to preach when the people want to hear them and preach when it seems they don't want to hear them.

We had been a long time where preaching was easy because it was in season. However, as soon as we run into a difficult season it appears, we run inside and hide from the demands of the vocation. One of which is being a preacher sometimes requires us to be in harms way. We do not do this negligently. We don't do it irresponsibly. But someone must accept the fact that preaching is not always in season.

The Apostles that paved the way for us never tapped out on the ministerial assignment because it was dangerous. They preached in the face of imminent death and ostracization. They preached pending severe beatings and prison sentences. They preached because necessity had laid it upon them to preach. They felt like Woe unto themselves if they declined preaching that Gospel.

We are out of season…but we still must be instant.

This is important for our discussion of this matter because to a great degree preachers and pastors have handled this pandemic much like our President has handled it…that is not handling it at all.

Number 45 has allowed his negligence to become dazzlingly brilliant as he simply plays down, or all together ignores the health crisis that we are in as a nation.

Donald Trump has gone on record sharing with pomposity and bombast that this pandemic is everything from fake news, to nothing to worry about. He said it would be over in a very short while. Now with election day 2020 rapidly approaching he is saying it is serious and we need to be careful. However, he makes these statements at a rally for his presidential run while addressing a substantial crowd of unmasked attendees. This is not just confusing, it is laughable.

So then, in an unwitting matter we speak out against the president, but we handle our churches, congregations and the bible the same way. With negligence and ignorance hoping it will just go away. But in the meantime, the churches are empty, and we are allowing an absence of corporate worship to become the new normal for the Body of Christ.

This is happening because we are moving in fear and not facts, or faith.

In this time of fear, we are telling ourselves whatever we need to hear in large doses to manufacture for our daily existence some type of normalcy. We want to believe that we are helping. We want to believe that we are in control, when clearly, we are not. It is this feeling of fear and not having control that makes us adopt absurdities as plausible and reasonable responses to things that are beyond our depth. Because we are moving in fear it places us further in harm's way.

The Today Show just aired a segment recently about native New Yorkers pulling up stakes and moving to Florida. The irony in this is New York was the original epicenter of the pandemic in the U.S. As of mid-August, California, Florida and Texas *have* surpassed New York for total cases to date, though New York still *has* the *highest* death total. People are not going to the states where coronavirus has been diagnosed the least like South Dakota, Utah, Oklahoma and Idaho, but they are moving to a pandemic hot spot to find refuge.

The cause of this is the fear factor that we have used to maneuver this terrible time in our history and now that people are petrified, they are doing what petrified people do. Panic and act unreasonably to the thing they fear.

This, in my opinion is the reason why faith, church, worship and prayer are so important to this particular moment in time. It will allow us to re-center ourselves and focus on things that encourage us and not those things that keep us heavy, discourage, depressed and divided.

Donald Trump is just now starting to acknowledge that we are in a serious place. However, this is probably more due to vote pandering than believing the science of this critical time in our country.

Lastly, I would like to say that when fear is used to control a body of people there are always those who are fearless. The fearless make it their business to double down on all things opposite to prove that the fear factor is indeed a farce. This makes for a greater cause of confusion and indifference to a very serious situation.

Because Church is a microcosm of the society at large, whatever is happening in a given community or even country is also happening in the Church. The people who occupy the community are the same people who also occupy our churches and they bring their fears and concerns with them.

So, we find ourselves confronted with three realities. There are those who will not return to church until Dr. Fauci himself is on every news outlet saying, "you may go back to church now". The other group is made up of those who are both reckless and ridiculous. They are functioning as if there is nothing of urgency going on and they are regularly placing themselves as well as others in harm's way.

Finally, there are those of us who find ourselves in the middle. We are trying our best to press forward, but we do so with caution and concern for ourselves and for others.

The cause of the chaos is twofold. There is a lack of unity on the matter and a lack of transparency. These two things alone are the recipe for chaos and disaster. Our own president has admitted that he did not tell the people earlier because he did not want the country to panic. In this day and age of information, information does not cause panic, it's what we crave for the most part to keep ourselves from fear and panic.

It has been the lack of information that has caused the panic. Because there were no definitive answers it pushed society to the place of extreme panic. Rations on water, toilet paper, paper towels and other things became an immediate issue because we were left by our government to our own imaginations.

Perhaps the most sobering thing in all this was not the shortage of paper products, but the shortage of handguns and weapons across the country. The nation was beginning to feel like the country could no longer protect us, so we made ourselves ready to protect our own…by any means necessary. This is a powder keg waiting to explode.

In this silence and confusion, the Church does not combat it, but we flow with it. When in fact, if we ever needed to hear from the Lord before, surely, we need to hear from the Lord right now.

We need direction for our families. We need direction for our finances. We need direction for our faith. We need direction on our fears. We need a word from the Lord. When people are troubled, panicked and afraid, silence is never golden. It becomes the very nudge that causes us to fall from the precipice of which we are trying so desperately to balance.

Proverbs 29:18
18 Where there is no vision, the people perish: but he that keepeth the law, happy is he.
KJV

The proverbial writer is sharing with us that in a time where there is no revelation or word being shared, or when people do not have clear instruction, they become loosened from their basic foundations in faith and rely on emotion and instinct. This can cause them to become undone in their disciplines of faith and virtue as a people.

Chapter 3
Knowing the Times

Hosea 4:6
6 My people are destroyed for lack of knowledge: because thou hast rejected knowledge, I will also reject thee, that thou shalt be no priest to me: seeing thou hast forgotten the law of thy God, I will also forget thy children.
KJV

So then, the charge is for every leader, teacher, minister, elder, pastor, preacher, bishop, apostle and officer of the Church of Jesus Christ to have something to say concerning the state of our nation and reconcile that to the Word of God.

This is a tall order considering the place that preaching is in right now. Gospel preaching is rare to hear now a days. As a scholar, teacher, professor, and bishop in the Lord's Church it is overwhelmingly disappointing to hear the preaching that is being done from week to week in the Kingdom. Because we have waved the rigors of training and discipline for the preacher. There is now a generation of preachers who mount the sacred desk every week without really knowing what it is they are talking about.

The preaching of the Gospel is never supposed to be our best effort at explaining what we got from passage we read over a few times. However, Gospel preaching is to be handled as a professional craft that it takes a lifetime to master. The disciplines of Hermeneutics and Homiletics should not be forgotten. Understanding the historical nuances of the ancient languages of Greek and Hebrew should not be dismissed. Having an understood call should not be trivialized. We still need men and women of God who know that they have been commissioned by God to share this Great Gospel.

To this end we are not permitted to simply give motivational talks. We are not allowed by the mandate of scripture to bend the sacred text so that it pleases the itching ears of this present age. We cannot satiate the lifestyles of a church gone wild with permissive preaching that accommodates sin as an understood and accepted lifestyle. We must preach the Gospel.

I would understand the negotiations of sacred text if in fact we understood it to be text that were attributed to human transmission. However, we understand it and deem it far much more than intellectuals throughout the ages coming together and giving erudite opinions concerning God, the Son of God, His Spirit and the Faith.

We believe it to be the inspired Word of God. This being the case, our task is not to negotiate what the word means in our present economy of morality. We must be disciplined to say what God said and to say it congruently to the best of our ability with what His intent was and is for His people.

Revelation 22:18-20

For I testify unto every man that heareth the words of the prophecy of this book, If any man shall add unto these things, God shall add unto him the plagues that are written in this book:

19 And if any man shall take away from the words of the book

of this prophecy, God shall take away his part out of the book of life, and out of the holy city, and from the things which are written in this book.
20 He which testifieth these things saith, Surely, I come quickly. Amen. Even so, come, Lord Jesus.
KJV

We have an obligation to make God's words our words. We do not have permission to make our words his words.

With great discipline and anguish the messenger of this Great Gospel; no matter the capacity you serve in, is to make certain that we share the sentiment and will of God to all mankind.

It appears that as we have made membership more important than discipleship, we clamor desperately to draw people to a facility that will house them and their preferences much more than to a faith that will change them and ready them to meet their God.

It is not my belief that this has been done maliciously or malevolently. I believe that the enemy has had us to arrive at this place surreptitiously across the canvas of the years. We are not being blindsided by this new fluid concept of preaching that so readily alienates true biblical interpretation. The truth of the matter is we were warned about it a long time ago:

Timothy 4:3-4
For the time will come when they will not endure sound doctrine; but after their own lusts shall they heap to themselves teachers, having itching ears;
4 And they shall turn away their ears from the truth, and shall be turned unto fables.
KJV

We cannot say that we were not warned about what we are witnessing as sound biblical preaching in these times. Paul makes it clear that preachers would in some way lose their integrity and begin to pander for the approval of people in a mass falling away from the faith in the likes of which the world has not seen until this present age.

We are in this place because somehow it became more important to be popular than to be effective. I do not know what caused the slippery slope. I do not know if it was the great awakenings that we experienced like Brother Seymore and Azusa Street, or the massive appeal of the Civil Rights struggle; but, somewhere in our rather recent history we began to be motivated by crowds and applause instead of the will of God.

Let us talk for a while and see if we can discuss what brought the church from being a powerful place that became popular, to a popular place that no longer has power.

Many would jump into the discussion here and begin to blame the preacher. We would blame pastors and men and women of God everywhere and say it is their fault for this place in which the Church has entered. While we do have blame to own, it is not 100% our fault. The Pauline text that we shared coming from II Timothy chapter 4 told us that the people would "heap to themselves" teachers who would tell them what they wanted to hear. This simply means that people would rather hear a convenient lie than a convicting truth.

The last I checked, church was still very much voluntary. In other words, we go where we like, and we go if we like. Therefore, the people in the pews are as much to blame as the preachers in the pulpit when it comes to the messages that are being preached. I cannot place you under arrest and make you stay and hear me preach week after week. I must develop a message that suits the palate of the people who are in attendance. That is why Paul said the people were heaping to themselves preachers that say what they want them to say. That means we will only place over us preachers who will scratch our itching ears with what we want to hear.

On the other hand, shame on us who will say anything to keep our church full, our closets deep, our cars gassed up and our egos stroked. Have we sold out this Great Gospel to have a "good life"?

I mean, what would happen to us if we still preached what the bible says about fornication, adultery, homosexuality and envy? What would happen to us if we told the truth about those who needed discipline before they ever walk in the rare air of Christian Leadership? What would happen to us if we actually spoke truth to power and that power was not the mayor or the president; but, that power was the people who write the biggest tithe checks in church.

It becomes impossible to challenge a criminal justice system when you refuse to even challenge your Minister of Music or other leaders in your congregation.

It is my sincere belief that many of us who preach have become hypercritical in our presentation of the Gospel because we have a fear of being normal.

The normal sized church in the United States of America is only about fifty people. So many of us would rather have a Hellish Full house than Holy Fifty. It is because of this that much of our preaching has become presentations that accommodate sin and indifference towards the Word of God rather than discipline that can change a generation into the Kingdom that God so desperately craves for us to be.

There may be some who take issue with me referencing God as being "desperate." To be clear the premise of salvation is rooted and grounded in the desperation that God felt for us as He witnessed Adam fall so far from him. What is sacrificing one's only begotten son other than desperation that is premised in a gargantuan love? God is desperate...but not in any lack of his own, because in him there is no failure. God finds his desperation in our negligence to be what He both designed and desires for us to be.

Just like any good parent God is desperately waiting for us to achieve obedience and purpose so that faith might become fruition.

This never became clearer to me than it did as I watched how the leadership of the Church of Jesus Christ handled this pandemic known to us as Covid-19.

The Church of Jesus Christ became just as inept and ignorant as the Trump administration in handling this situation. We waited to hear from a divided and diluted government instead of turning to the Word of the Lord. Here in our state of Ohio, the governor never made it mandatory that churches would close.

There were a couple of times where he suggested and/ or recommended it, but he never mandated it. I must say that I appreciated Governor Mike DeWine for that. There seemed to be a part of him even in this global crisis that trusted the spiritual leadership to lead. Because of that I am hopeful.

There are also men and women of God, pastors, who could not participate in corporate worship because they had compromised immune systems. I understand them staying at home and staying safe, but what I do not understand is missing the opportunity to train up leadership to stand in your stead during this time of crisis.

We struggle with this greatly in the Black Church Experience. Our congregations almost refuse to hear anyone but the pastor on a regular basis. However, a great part of development is practicing the trade you are seeking to develop.

While many pastors act like it is a burden to have congregations who only desire to hear us, the truth of the matter is many of us relish the sentiment. It does wonders for our egos. Perhaps what we are missing is the fact that it cripples the church. We should constantly be developing leadership for the next generational assignment of the church. A succession plan is necessary for every church.

One of the greatest things I remember about growing up in Youngstown, Ohio was it being a church town. With the loss of industry and the perpetual battle of poverty, Youngstown is now known as the "Incredible Shrinking City". This moniker was given to us by a documentarian who shared that in the last several census that have been taken Youngstown has shrank in its population each time.

It is noticeable as you see blighted neighborhoods on every side of town and once booming factories either totally shut down or only a fragment of what they once were. Be that as it may, there was a time when Youngstown, Ohio was indeed a church town. All the churches were filled of every denomination and ethnic culture. I had friends in school that were church kids like me. We did not have to hide our faith, but we could wear it in school and for the most part, we were respected for being young people of faith.

The great part about that is my friends came from other denominations. What I noticed about my friends in the COGIC (Church Of God In Christ) is they had great depth in their music department.

Two of my closest friends growing up were exceptional musicians. Sometimes I would be privileged to go to church with them on Friday nights or perhaps Sunday evenings. What I noticed was them being late did not stop worship service from starting.

There were always younger kids who would get on the instruments and play until they got there. Service would continue and the those who were learning would carry service until the designated leadership arrived.

We don't see much of that anymore. We need to get back to the place of developing young leaders in church who are well able to conduct all facets of church even if they do not function in the top tier of leadership.

We should be following the leadership paradigm that the Lord Jesus Christ set up for his church. The Lord built a church that could function, develop and grow without his physical presence being there. He not only expected for the church to survive without his physical presence. He expected the church to thrive without his physical presence and it did. Reference John chapter 14.

To any pastor reading this who has a ministry that will not function, develop and grow without your physical presence, you have done an ineffective job developing leaders in your ministry. Church should go on even if we can't make it. There should always be people in place to carry on at the same level, if not greater.

John 14:12
Verily, verily, I say unto you, He that believeth on me, the works that I do shall he do also; and greater works than these shall he do; because I go unto my Father.
KJV

Chapter 4
Knowing the Effects

Post-modernity has already done a job on the Church of Jesus Christ. Allow me to share at the onset of this chapter that I am not of the mindset that the Church is doing a capitol job in her existence in the earth. I am much more cynical and skeptical about the current status of the Body of Christ.

I see all the headway that we have made achieving things that can be measured with secular gauges. There are the phenomenal buildings that we have erected. There is the colossal presence we have on television and social media. We can also reference the temporal gain that we have amassed for ourselves. Despite these things, we still must ask the question, are we any better?

Not do we feel better about ourselves, but I am asking the question are we any better as Ambassadors of Jesus Christ?

Do we have more anointing?

Do we possess more Holy Ghost authority?

Is our witness stronger in the earth?

Are our messages preached with demon chasing power?

This question must be asked and answered as we stand in the face of such a challenging time. Are we ministering with cutting edge effectiveness or are we just going through the ecclesiastical and liturgical motions?

This is a necessity because as we are confronted with the

nuances and premises of Post-Modernity the message of the Gospel is on the line. Post-Modern meaning the time after the Modernity which can be documented as mid 20th century and beyond. Postmodernism represents the place of no assumed certainty of scientific, or objective efforts. It represents both a liquid and ever emerging scrutiny for everything that is thought to be concrete.

In this chapter we want to identify several key problems that Post-Modernity creates for the Church.

This age in which we preach continues to negotiate their salvation as opposed to receiving their salvation. Those who are reading this came to Jesus on His terms. There was no negotiating, there were no platforms to stand on, we come from a premise of preaching that embodied the Phrase "Holiness or Hell."

Most of us had literal "church clothes" because church attendance was a value, not an option.

We come from the place where sin was sin and even some things that were not sin were sin depending on what denomination you emanated from.

However, in this emerging church we can now negotiate salvation almost as if we are negotiating the terms on a car or a house. We are literally living in an age that is trying to reassess and reinterpret the timeless text known as the Bible to suit temporal agendas.

This is Post-Modern thought, and it is the time that has produced the Millennials. This is what it causes us to do:

› We are redefining whether it is okay for a Christian couple to shack up.
› We are redefining the very sacred interpretations of

marriage and sexuality.
- We are redefining what family is.
- We are redefining what worship looks like and even what Gospel preaching sounds like.
- We are redefining what Christian socialization looks like.

Why are we reinterpreting the sacred scriptures?

- The current Post-Modern society does not like hard lines of demarcation.
- The current Post-Modern society believes that right and wrong are subjective fluid concepts.
- The current Post-Modern society does not like any kind of hierarchal authority.
- The current Post-Modern society is inclined to believe that even God should meet them half-way.

A great number of church leaders in the 21st century are stuck between two worlds. The people who raised us in ministry are from a period heavily influenced by the industrial age in our country. The people that we minister to are from this current age of Technology. We who lead them are old enough to remember structure and not quite young enough to appreciate the freedom technology fosters.

The effect that this has had on the Body of Christ has been enormous. Before the Church was ever confronted with the realities of Covid-19 we were already struggling with both identity and growth. Most of us don't need researchers such as the Barna Group to tell us that church attendance has been cut more than 50% in the last twenty years. We can gauge that difference very easily with a simple eyeball test. As I travel the country preaching and teaching most agree that the churches that were all filled to capacity 20-30 years ago are all less than half-full now.

We have done all we know to do to stop the proverbial hemorrhaging of congregants, but nothing has really helped us.

We have tried to make the church as sinner friendly as possible, but in doing so almost no modern church facility looks like a place of worship at all. We now offer strobe lighting, theater seating, come as you are dressing, contemporary singing and re-imagined lifestyle and living; but none of these things separately or all together have worked to cause people to return to the church for worship service. I have seen coffee shops and eateries right in the vestibule of the facility and that still does not guarantee attendance.

So, in short, we have traded all things sacred and or traditional for all things contemporary and in some cases profane to assure attendance, but the reality is the Church in America is still shrinking drastically. Whatever shall we do about our numbers in attendance and participation?

This is an urgent question we must ask because coming out of this pandemic will not make church as we know it any easier. To the contrary, church will become exponentially more difficult to facilitate and present.

When this virus began to permeate our country I immediately turned to God for help. As I stated in the opening pages, we had just embarked on a brand-new reformation in the country. I am the president of our accredited bible college. We have a 501c3 that is viable and operable to the communities in which our churches and partners exist. We have two campuses in northeast Ohio in the cities of Barberton and Youngstown.

I needed to hear from God on whether I should close the church for the duration or continue to function and keep a modified version of our ministry going as we wade through the very murky and uncertain waters of this international crisis.

To be clear, I did not know what to do. As a senior pastor and now Bishop in the Lord's Church I did not know what to do. I have six degrees to my academic credit which include an earned doctorate, but I still did not know what to do. I had been preaching and pastoring for more than thirty years and yet, I did not know what to do.

When I found myself totally ignorant of what to do, I got on my face and I began to pray and seek the Lord. I was not doing this for the Body of Christ. I was only doing it for the 400-500 people that call me their leader. This number includes my family. I needed to know what me and my house were supposed to do.

I am suggesting to every pastor who may be reading this to make certain before you ask your colleagues what they are doing, ask God what He is requiring from you first in any ministerial moment. It is important for us to not do what is popular, or even normal. We must do what it is we hear God directing us to do. Once we make the decision to go with what God has instructed and commissioned us to do, we trust Him and move forward in that.

The Christian Revival & Discipleship Center (Christ Centered Church) is a very peculiar church. We have a lot of people in our church at the two campuses that do not possess a traditional church pedigree. In fact, many of our adult parishioners will tell you that Christ Centered Church is the first church they have ever belonged to in their lives or at the very least to which they have been committed.

These people whom I love as a brother but lead as an assignment come from every challenging walk of life you could imagine. The

Lord told me they would not do well if they could not come to the physical place of worship. The Lord instructed me that many would turn back if we forsook assemblage for a season. So, just like that I had an assignment to keep church open, but to do so with stipulations and changes that would help us in the transition and even growth after the pandemic stopped.

Once I got my assignment, I then needed tutoring. I called one of my big brothers in the ministry to ask what he was doing. He instructed me on what methods he was using for worship and I heard the Spirit of the Lord say to me as plain as day, "You do likewise."

Here's what we did. We had to make adjustments for both safety and common sense:

- All weekly meetings and rehearsals were stopped including bible study and Sunday School.
- We suspended all choir singing and rehearsal.
- We only had one service per week on Sunday for 1hr.
- We sat 6 ft apart…every other row.
- We made masks mandatory in the worship experience.
- We had them available to pass out to those who did not have one.
- We stopped communion services until further notice.
- We developed two crews to sanitize and clean church weekly.
- We hired a company to sanitize professionally.
- We suspended altar appeals and corporate prayer at the altar.
- We would only have the church open for that 1hr per week to maintain a sanitized meeting place.
- I restricted attendance to only those who were not at high

risk for contracting the virus. The others I admonished to stay home and watch on social media.
› We took temperatures at the door and had people who entered sign wavers who did not have a fever. Those with even low-grade fevers were sent home.

This has been our protocol and God has been faithful. We have not had one case of COVID-19 that has been contracted at our church. God has been extremely kind. I thank God for what He has used us to do.

However, it was about three months into our pandemic protocol that God began to speak to me again. He told me to not change the worship format that He had given to us. He told me that this is what His Church would look like for us moving forward.

Church that we had developed over the years had become full of pageantry and regalia. We were celebrating people more than we had been celebrating God or His Son that died for us. God told me to streamline the services coming out of the pandemic so that it would be easy for people to find him in the worship moment.

Some of us had forgotten that it is His house!!!

We moved all the furnishings of man out of the worship experience so that it would be easy for people to find the Lord instead of our furnishings. Here's what worship for us looks like now:

A Call To Worship......Elder
Congregational Song
Scripture/Prayer
Congregational Song
Preached Word
Closing Prayer & Dismissal: *(offering to be given while*

exiting)

This service takes us 50 – 65 minutes. Since we have been using our abbreviated services we have added to our church membership over 20 people during this time of pandemic. God has been a WONDER!!!

It was frightening to do, but God honored our obedience and we have been blessed for taking the risk He told us to take and stay open. Our offerings have increased during this season and we average over 1400 views per week of our worship service on Sunday and our midweek teaching on Wednesdays that we do on Facebook Live. The number of people we are reaching has tripled in these seven months of social distancing and God has given us a formula that will indeed minister to this present age.

Please make sure to understand that I could not read this in a book. I got this the old-fashioned way of laying on my face, hearing from God and then trusting Him to be faithful. Now that I have heard from him, I'm simply sharing with you what He gave to us in hopes that it can at the very least inspire you.

I cannot say that God will tell you to do what I did. I do know for certain that if you do what He tells you to do for your congregation and family He will bless you and cover you in your obedience to him.

Chapter 5
Knowing the Cost

Everyone will never be on board.

I had to learn early on that if I were to be obedient to the voice of God, it would call me into question with man.

In the Church we love to quote faith texts and tell the people about faith and how we trust God. The only problem with that is the Church of Jesus Christ is not supposed to just talk about faith. We are supposed to live it in our daily existence.

Romans 1:17
For therein is the righteousness of God revealed from faith to faith: as it is written, The just shall live by faith.
KJV

When we say that we are supposed to "live by faith." What does that mean? Well, the word in the New Testament is *pistis*. This word means to believe in God strongly that He is able to save you. To be fully persuaded of that one thing in such a way that it causes you to live differently.

My faith in essence is supposed to navigate my life. Because of my faith I am pushed in directions that I wouldn't normally go in, but my faith has the final say so in my life. Therefore, as I navigate the sea of life I am pushed by a rudder of faith and guided by compass of obedience. That faith causes me to make decisions that may not be popular, but they keep me in the will of God. Me being in the will of God is what makes me "just."

I am not "just" or "justified" because I say so, but I am justified because my life moves say so. My very movement in life emanates from my very faith in God. I am fully persuaded that God will save me and that because He has saved me, He will in fact take care of me, or provide for me. This is pisteuo in the original language. He is not just a God who saves me and then leaves me to fend for myself. He is a God who saves me and then provides for me as I am determined to honor Him with my life or be "just" because of my position in Him.

The majority of believers are not here for that! We have been given a faith that tells us God simply appeases us and blesses us where we are and how we are. And we omit the challenge of discipleship which is what causes us to be just.

Many will never know what it is for the Lord to truly provide because they have never truly had to trust Him for provision. When I step out on or, in faith it pushes me to the place of total dependence upon the God which I say told me to step out in first place.

When you are a person of this kind of faith and move towards God in your behavior, many will not celebrate you, they will criticize your actions as being both fanatical and dangerous. You could very easily become an outcast from the very church that you love so much.

Many of us in the Body of Christ love to have what I call a hyperbolic relationship with the Lord. It is not pragmatic or factual. It is more so exaggerated and pretentious. Hyperbole becomes the way in which we communicate our faith. It is always outstanding and animated. It is always the absolute rave when we speak of it, but it is rarely seen as we live from day to day. To exercise faith in this world is to become ostracized for doing so.

Therefore, we live by the old adage, "let's not, but say we did". Let's not trust him but tell everyone we did. Let's not believe scripture but tell everyone we do. Let's not bend our lives towards him but tell everyone we have. This is an existence that becomes a hyperbolic display at best because we fear losing the approval of those who surround us.

Ladies and gentlemen please believe me, the most sobering thing about ministry in the last thirty years has been standing alone. It is remarkable how many times people will say they believe what you believe, and they embrace what you embrace yet leave you standing alone when the rubber meets the road. This is the cost, and you should know it moving forward that standing on the word and will of God in trying times will absolutely leave you standing alone with the Lord.

Here are some names to consider:

Abram/Abraham, Noah, Rahab, Shadrach, Meshack, Abednego, Esther, Jacob, Joseph, David, Peter, Paul, Anna, Mary and Jesus.

This is a very short list of people who all found themselves standing alone in scripture. Please note that this list is not exhaustive. There are many more who stood alone. This is just a list to get us thinking of how normal it is to become ostracized because of the faith you are attempting to live by and not just simply talk about.

To become faith driven many times means to denounce the positions and accolades of men to do the will and the work of God. Please do not expect to be both purposeful and popular in this world.

When we made the announcement to stay open during the pandemic, we were met with sharp criticism from everyone. Some of the people were genuinely concerned for our safety. However, others were simply judgmental because us being open convicted them about being closed.

It was said that we were putting our people in harm's way. It was said that we were just doing it for the money or the offerings. It was even said that we were doing it to satisfy our own ego. In fact, it was none of that. I simply heard the Lord say, "stay open."

It is a concern that church has moved to a place where if it causes us any inconvenience or sacrifice then we deem it the devil.

I challenge everyone reading this right now to consider where the faith we embrace was birthed from. From Genesis to Revelation, we see people of the faith and the Body of Christ in harm's way. We see brothers and sisters persecuted in every genre of scripture. Somehow, we've come to this place of faith where we believe that our obstacles and enemies should only be those that we can bear.

The truth of the matter is salvation has always been dirty work. We must extend this faith to those in need not only in times of convenience, but when it is the most inconvenient to do so. This is the call that we have on our lives as the Church of Jesus Christ.

Was I afraid? Yes. But not enough to trade the peace of God for a spirit of fear. Was I concerned? Yes. But not enough to stop casting my cares upon him because I know he cares for me.

I am by no means saying that those of us who stayed open were functioning on a higher plain of spirituality than those who did not stay open. I am saying whether you stayed open or not, be able to say that you did so because that's what you clearly heard God tell you to do.

Now, be very sure that I am challenging you if your decision was a knee-jerk response to the news or peer pressure from other pastors and leaders to never let that happen again. God has been too good to all of us for us to make decisions because of what man says. We owe it to God and the people He has made us responsible for to lay on our faces before Him and let him give us the direction in which we are to go.

Be very sure that those directions will be different paths to same place of obedience. Be that as it may, it will result in his will instead of our worry.

Chapter 6
Knowing the Fears

---

2 Timothy 2:15
15 Study to shew thyself approved unto God, a workman that needeth not to be ashamed, rightly dividing the word of truth.
KJV

The Lord's idea of Church was never to build an address. The Lord's idea of Church was for Church to be perpetually expansive. He was never interested in building a building, that's why He took his ministry out of the building. He was interested in building people. So, he left erected buildings and established architecture and went to find crushed people.

His plan for us was to make sure that there was "us" everywhere. He wanted believers and disciples in every walk of life. We only want believers and disciples at our address, to build our ministry, to raise our offerings and to assert our agenda. This is the opposite of the plan of The Church that Jesus left.

Churches are not shrinking across the country because the Devil is busy. Churches are shrinking across the country because we have not changed the actual foundation of the model of church since industrialization or perhaps even earlier. Church must become what is necessary right now.

Therefore, there is a need for Gospel Preaching. However,

Gospel Preaching does not just cover the birth, the life, the death, the burial, the resurrection, the ascension and the second coming of Jesus Christ. It must cover people in their very real dilemmas. This is the preaching demographic. Gospel Preaching must cover who Jesus would cover:

Jesus embraced who they rejected.

It is not our job to become the Holy Ghost for people. We do not save anybody. Our job is to love them and then inform them. It is not up to us to decide who can come in and who cannot. Our job is to love them unconditionally and then preach unadulteratedly. Between these two dynamics the Lord will save them and change them if He desires their change. Never is it the job of the church to affirm anyone in their lifestyle or, condemn anyone in their lifestyle. We love them, we instruct them, the Lord and the Holy Ghost handles the rest.

Jesus went where they would not go.

Go Get'em!!! That's the last thing Jesus said to his disciples. I need you to go out and find the people and get them. As you get them, teach them and usher them into a relationship of faith with God through me. Go get them. You cannot wait for them to come to you, you go get them.

One of the greatest mistakes of the church is that we stopped going to get people. We have made it our posture to just acquire property, hang signage and then open the doors. "If you build it, they will come…" or "build it and they will come…" was never the slogan of the church. The church was always premised in building people not things. Have we become more interested in things than souls???

Jesus said a truth that was not popular to say.
Truth is always dogmatic. Truth does not change. Truth is always just that, the truth. In post modern times we like to encourage people to live their truth, or speak their truth. I do not believe it to be prudent or helpful for the church of Jesus Christ to embrace the notion that there are multiple truths. Usually, there are multiple facts, but you can only have one truth.

I don't have the time to write about it, but I'll just say multiple truths is what leaves us with George Floyd, Breonna Taylor, Ahmad Arbery and so many others…the legal system went with another truth…

The truth is sometimes hard to hear, but Jesus promises it will always emancipate us. Truth and Love is a powerful cocktail.

Jesus also suffered where many wanted prosperity.
The notion that I can live for Christ and never suffer is ridiculous. There is a level of hurt that automatically comes with being born again, a Christian leader, a gospel preacher, a pastor etc.

Jesus called us to be witnesses. That word in the original language is phonetically (mar toos). It's where we get our English word martyr. Martyr means to be one who dies for a cause. Jesus is literally calling us to die to our agenda and become alive to his. The problem is…nobody wants to die.

Jesus left the Temple to do ministry in the woods.
It was not just radical for Jesus and John the Baptist to be in the woods, it was necessary for survival. They could not do what they were doing under the watchful eyes of Jewish leadership that had been bought and paid for by the Roman government. So, they did ministry out in the woods. However, they never boycotted

traditional worship. Jesus attended church and even taught there.

On two very special occasions Jesus even fought at church. The Church is the equivalent to the locker room. Life is the field of play. You can never win if we don't see what you can do outside of the locker room. Come join us on the field of play.

These are the basic tenants of Gospel Preaching explained in short. The purpose of preaching is to impact people. The purpose of impacting people is to impact families. The purpose of impacting families is to impact communities. The purpose of impacting communities is to impact societies. The purpose of impacting societies is to impact the country. The purpose of impacting the country is to impact the world. The purpose of impacting the world is to advance the Kingdom of God.

But all this starts with the preacher being able to connect with a person.

Preaching is done for the purpose of saving souls. Souls are saved for the purpose of making disciples.

When Jesus left the disciples for the last time, He charged them with an assignment of Kingdom Expansion. It was their sole duty to advance the Kingdom. His very clear and definitive directive was to go and make disciples. They were supposed to do this by teaching them whatever He had taught them and baptizing them.

The emphasis that the Lord gave them on teaching cannot be exaggerated. It is important for us to grasp the fact that disciples are not born, they are made. They are made through instruction, prayer, rebuke and encouragement. The making of a disciple should never be looked at as an event. It is definitely a process. Believers are born (Born Again), disciples are made.

As the Kingdom expands it will require a different kind of leader and personnel. As long as they are not far from Jerusalem

Jesus knows Peter will be sufficient. His very direct approach to preaching is appropriate for the audiences that he will face. However, as the church grows, and the Kingdom begins to reach places that are far from Jerusalem even though they may be occupied by Jews another type of voice is needed.

Paul is not the unsophisticated voice of a working-class fisherman. Paul is a polished scholar who understands both Roman and Jewish law. Paul is eloquent and articulate, and it appears that Paul is who God actually wanted to replace Judas Iscariot.

Jesus already had his ranks full of men who could minister to the immediate surroundings of Jerusalem. He did not have someone for the utter most part of the world. He had those who could minister effectively to the Jews, but He did not have one who could do so with the gentiles. This is the call of Paul.

Consider Paul's credentials:
> Educated by Gamaliel
> Paul had dual citizenship
> Paul was a Pharisee
> Paul was on the Sanhedrin Court
> Paul had military experience
> Paul had experience in other cultures

It is clear, God is not about to change the message of salvation. He is not even changing the method of salvation. But God is indeed changing the medium of salvation as it relates to personnel.

We must be clear in this present age that there is more than one way to get the message of Jesus Christ out. It is the challenge of every minister, elder, preacher or pastor to be certain that they are as prolific as possible in as many ways to present as possible so that the message of salvation will not suffer because of our personal style.

There are many ways to convey the message:

> *Whoop it out* – there are a plethora to think of. This is the bedrock tradition of the African American preaching experience. When done correctly it is nothing short of heavenly. When done, it is egregious to say the least. Whooping is a very melodic way of preaching the gospel. The historians call it sing/song method. For this you need to have a melodious voice and at least be able to stay on key. In many instances, a gifted musician can help you develop this style. While it is considered old school, whooping still works if you know how to do it.

> *Cadence it out* – Think Dr. Martin Luther King Jr. He was the absolute King of Cadence. Dr. King, with his billowing and haunting voice, used cadence to create excitement. While it is not as melodious as whooping, cadence relies on timing and rhythm to be un-relinquishing.

> *Teach it out* – think about the preaching styles of Charles Stanley, Tony Evans or Joyce Meyer, Myles Munroe. Just stand flat footed and be able to rightly divide the word of truth line upon line and precept upon precept so that the people leave with understanding.

> *Lecture it out* – Literally become a teacher and or professor and teach the word of God with clarity, conviction, and

boldness.

› *Write it out* – become an author or one who prepares lessons for Sunday school or training.

› *Sing it out* – This is what all of our Gospel artists are doing. It still the word!!!

› *Tweet it out* – Social media is a legitimate form of conveying the gospel message of salvation. If you don't speak it, you better find someone who does so that your church, your message and your mission will remain relevant.

The assignment of the preacher is not about what we desire, it's about where we are needed. While it is voluntary, it is still very much necessity driven. God says will anyone go for us…and we reply here am I, send me. The assignment is not just an idea, but it is an organic pull and burden that will not release us.

Whether Old Testament or New Testament, the assignment is never about the individual, it's about the Will of God or the advancement of the Kingdom happening because of the individual being yielded. So many of us settle for building churches, careers and ministries as opposed to building and advancing the Kingdom. Let God develop you how He wants to and use you where He wants to.

Chapter 7
Knowing the Demographic

We are in a very pressing time as Christian leaders. The society at large is in constant turmoil. The world is constantly searching for answers. They are so overwhelmed that they will almost turn to anyone or anything to try and get some relief from what life is doing to them.

This is a very vulnerable place to be in. It is our responsibility as leaders, preachers and teachers to have something of substance to say to them that will help them through this unavoidable period in their lives.

As I stated in a previous chapter, our church family has been very fortunate as it relates to Covid-19. God has truly honored our decision to trust Him. We have only had five cases between the two campuses and none of the cases have been church related. Also, everyone has recovered from the virus. To God be the Glory!!!

However, watching the reality of this is very sobering. Everyone does not have that testimony. I have still had to officiate funerals during this time and some of those funerals have been for people who were claimed by this dreaded disease. It is incredibly difficult to grieve while social distancing.

One of the first funerals I did back in March was my nephew. Only 33 years old, but between his asthma and the virus he died reaching for his inhaler in a panic.

The funeral services were unbelievably difficult. Only thirty people of our very large family were able to attend due to the pandemic protocol that the funeral home was observing. There was to be no touching or hand shaking or sitting next to each other. It was unbearable to watch the pain and brokenness in my brother's eyes as he buried his only son and could not receive the intimacy necessary to heal and recover from such a devastation.

Families all over the world have been dealing with this all year. The holidays are quickly approaching. Seats will be empty at these Thanksgiving and Christmas festivities. Some because loved ones have died. Others will be vacant because we are looking at the harsh realities of having to cancel the holidays at our homes, considering that numbers are climbing throughout our country.

Suicide rates are increasing, and depression is becoming normal. People are having a difficult time managing the isolation of the pandemic. Many of our seniors have been placed on a proverbial island and they are not technologically savvy enough to connect through all the social media that is available. And moreover, countless numbers of neighborhood businesses are closing because they do not have the resources to float their small businesses through a pandemic.

All these reasons and more are why we cannot come at them with rhetoric or legalism when it's preaching time. We must be able to masterfully share our faith through application of the Word of God.

The key is we must do it as close to being without error as possible. The only way this can happen is if we take time to improve and enhance our interpretative and application skills concerning the Word of God.

This gives us another type of power in the lives of the people.

A power that is not there to control them to live for our various churches as much as it is there to free them so that they can live for Christ.

It is in this chapter that I intend to transfer this power to you by giving you some basic and simple disciplines that will help you become the leader, preacher, or teacher that God is calling for in this season of both urgency and accuracy.

The thing that I ask before we proceed is that you rid yourselves of any presuppositions concerning studying and applying the Word of God. I am certain that if you try to enter this experience as a blank slate God will richly bless you in this exercise. You will find that most of what you believe will be confirmed. It will only be enhanced by what I am trying to impart to you.

Let's get started.

Hermeneutics

Hermeneutics is the science of Scripture and or Bible interpretation. It is important for the serious Bible student to understand that it is a *science* and not an *art*. Because it is a science that means the interpreter is bound by certain rules of engagement as they approach the text that is to be interpreted. Here are some of those rules:
- There must be a belief that the Word of God is true.
- There must be a respect for the truth that is in the Word of God.
- The purpose of the study is truth not justification.
- The interpretation is bound by time, culture, and geography.
- The interpretation is the foundation of the application.
- If the interpretation is not accurate than the application is inaccurate.

Hermeneutics is not only important to preaching and teaching, but hermeneutics is important to Christian living. If I have been exposed to preaching that is premised in a bad hermeneutic it will then cause me to live out my faith in error. Many preachers, teachers, and leaders are guilty of sharing lessons and sermons that are premised in a bad hermeneutic and causing people to go out and try to live according to something that God has never actually said.

Dr. I. T. Bradley says, "It is important for us to know that God does not need us to talk about him, but he needs us to prepare ourselves so that He can talk about himself through us."

Therefore, the preaching and teaching dynamic is not about us being right as much as it is about the truth of God being exposed to those who would hear it, even if we cannot explain the truth in detail that is being exposed.

God can say something about himself that we cannot explain or that defies our standard of reasoning. Because this happens does not mean that God didn't say it. The word of God clearly tells us that He will at times confound the wise.

I Corinthians 1:27-29

"But God hath chosen the foolish things of the world to confound the wise ; and God hath chosen the weak things of the world to confound the things which are mighty; And base things of the world, and things which are despised, hath God chosen, yea, and things which are not, to bring to nought things that are: That no flesh should glory in his presence."
KJV

It is my sincere belief that anyone who is trying to understand

God's word from a truthful and sincere perspective must possess the following books in their library.

1. Strong's Exhaustive Concordance of the Bible
2. Biblical Hermeneutics (J. Edwin Hartill)
3. Ryrie's Systematic Theology (Charles Ryrie)
4. Life Application Study Bible (Personal Preference)
5. Nelson's Bible Dictionary (Personal Preference)
6. Nave's Bible Handbook (Personal Preference)
7. Bible Atlas
8. Dictionary of the Old Testament
9. Dictionary of the New testament

You can get all of these in hardcopy or you can purchase one good Bible program for your computer that will have all of these on it plus many more reference and study materials.

Because this is a book and not an actual Hermeneutics course I will not get into the finer points of this topic. It could never be done in a chapter. This information is given to you so you can begin to discipline yourself in the science of Bible interpretation on your own with the basics. It will be impossible to even begin to understand any text without having these basic tools available to you.

In this chapter I am going to share with you some very practical things that will take your preaching, teaching, and understanding to a whole new level. It is now important for us to explain to you that this is a chapter that will highlight expository preaching. Which means this is the discipline of exposing a given text. That means after we share the scripture everything else that is said from that point on will be in the text or directly related to the text.

It should be known that expository preaching is in fact the most effective form of preaching in terms of sharing Bible Truth. It is also the form of preaching if done correctly that gives the least margin of error when preaching. To be wrong in expository preaching means that the expositor has deliberately ignored a rule of interpreting the text. It should be further noted that this is very rarely done because the expositor is evil. It is however, more so done because of issues like tradition or even laziness.

Sometimes we will preach what we've heard instead of what we've found. The reason we will do this is because it is easier to *restate* information than it is to research the information. Preaching is no place for lazy people!!!

This being the case, let's discipline ourselves to do the following as expositors:

Pray

We must stop simply looking for good things to preach from week to week. It is important for every preacher/pastor to have a prayer life that is effective so that God can lead us in the proper direction concerning our sermonic choices. Praying is not just necessary for the topic, but even for the method in which we will present. We must hear God on whether we should leave the people of God celebrative, contemplative, or motivated.

This is NOT an endeavor we can approach without praying.

Choose texts not topics. (allow the text to give you your topics)

The expositor is not sitting somewhere pondering cool things to preach about. However, because of the study life of the expositor there are texts that we have studied and explored. These texts contain the topics that will be covered. We allow the text to produce the topic. We never superimpose a topic on a text.

Read the text until the story is fluent for you.

Familiarity with the text is important for anyone who is serious about preaching and teaching. If one is preaching about the Red Sea crossing found in Exodus, it is of paramount importance that the expositor become fluid in the dynamics of the epic we are attempting to narratively expose. In other words, KNOW THE WHOLE STORY!!!

Your text should be 10 verses or less even if the story is larger.

It is necessary for us to resist the temptation of reading too much scripture. Try to cut the text down to only read the section of the story that you are intending to expose. To read more than that is time consuming and it misleads the congregation. Never read scripture you have no intention of preaching or teaching.

Pull out all the significant words in phrases in the text.

Every significant word in the text should be isolated and underlined. These words of emphasis are necessary to find the intent of the author. We must stay connected to the original truth of the text. We cannot change it to ours. The Key Word Study Bible is a great addition to your library. It does this work for you.

Do a word study on these words.

Each of these words need to be looked up in their original language. If you are in the Old Testament it will be Hebrew. If you are in the New Testament it will Greek or Aramaic. For accuracy we must know what the words mean when they were written, not what they mean now.

Do a study on the book the text comes from.

The book of the Bible itself needs to be understood so that we can know the time and culture in which the passage was generated. These things will help us discover the mood of the text and the intent of the message being conveyed in the Bible.

Do a study on the culture that is dominant in the text.

When John tells us in the fourth chapter of his Gospel that Jesus is on his way to Samaria and is about to walk through it. There are cultural factors at play with that entire scriptural exchange between the woman at the well and Jesus. We need to know what those are before we attempt to construct any type of message.

Do a study on the geographical location.

When studying a text like the 23rd Psalm it is necessary to understand all the geographical nuances that are in that psalm. Understanding that exposes the text and the intent of the writer all the more.

Do a study on the main characters in the text.

When preaching a text, the expositor needs to deconstruct every personality in the text. I need to strip them down to their barest person-hood and let who they are at their core breathe. It is almost always relevant to how we interpret the text.

Highlight your theme, title, and points of emphasis.

Once I was in a conversation with Pastor John P. Kee. We were listening to someone sing. The person was a great singer, but Pastor Kee said something profound. He said, "Paramore, singing is like preaching…you can't get in the middle of a run and try to figure out where you're going with the run. You have to hear it before you land there."

We should never get up and just meander and talk. We must know where we're going before we ever get there. It's intentional.

Make an outline.

Many people don't like manuscript preachers. They say we are reading and not preaching. However, some of our most prolific preachers are manuscript preachers, and they do a phenomenal job both preparing and presenting their manuscripts.

My father in ministry, Dr. Roderick C. Pounds Sr., made us write out our messages word for word. He would say, "If you can write it, you can preach it!" I think it is important for young preachers/new preachers to be able to construct an entire manuscript and be able to preach from it. I think my success in ministry has a great deal to do with me learning early how to write a manuscript, and then as Dr. Pounds would say, "…get it off the page!!!" meaning preach it, don't read it.

However, if you are training preachers and you don't like manuscripts, at least make them do a full outline. This does two things; it gives us a record of what was preached, and it helps us develop our ability to think succinctly.

Once this is done, we must begin to package the message in a way that it is accurate, memorable, effective, and applicable.

I must listen for God to give me the correct application for the interpretation that I have realized. If the application is not both relevant and relative to my life the preaching will do me no good. It is the job of every expositor to make certain that the application is just as powerful as the interpretation.

When this happens, people look at the scripture as being relevant to their existence. It makes Bible reading and studying a necessity. It makes church a very crucial part of their lives. If we miss in this it will not just cause people to walk away from preaching, but it could very well cause people to walk away from church and perhaps even Jesus Christ himself as a real option for their existence.

The reason we preach a message must be deeper than it just being a good message to preach. The message must meet the people in the congregation right where they are. It must cause them to believe that God is present and alive in the very dynamic that they are living through. They must believe that not only is God present, but He cares about what they care about. He is concerned about what troubles them. And his desire is to help them become the very best version of themselves that they could possibly be.

This is exposing the saving power of Christ to them and this is the only reason we preach. We proclaim that Christ does not just save their souls, but He saves all of them in an effort to use them in the up building of the Kingdom of God.

My interpretation has to be so clear that my application cannot be argued with. When this happens the end result should produce motivation to live for Christ daily.

To motivate them I must lay before the Lord constantly to hear a new way to encourage them each week.

Ladies and gentlemen, brothers and sisters we are in a pandemic. We are suffering through a worldwide crisis. The preaching we do must encourage, enlighten, challenge and congratulate people each and every week. They need to know that we see them, we feel for them and most importantly God has a message for them that will help them navigate their situation safe until as Bishop Clifton Jones says, "their now becomes their next!!!"

Here's a list of sermons and bible studies I've presented during the pandemic. This list is to give you an idea of the texts and topics that God gave me to keep the people I lead motivated and faithful to God. They have even led some to Christ during the pandemic. Perhaps some of them will help you.

1. Nothing's Too Hard for God (Jeremiah 32:27 & 42)
2. Keep Moving Forward (Joshua 1:1-4)
3. Praising God in Peculiar Places (Psalm 34:1-8)
4. Lord Open Our Eyes (II Kings 6:8-17)
5. Open Doors (Revelation 3:8)
6. The Weight of Being A Witness (Revelation 11:3-12)
7. Breaking the Spell (Acts 8:5-12)
8. Changing the Face Of The Church (Luke 14:16-24)
9. Making Praise from Scratch (II Thessalonians 5:16-18)
10. Chasing Jesus (Mark 6:38)
11. A Muted Man (Matthew 9:32-33)

So, let's work on it…

Exercise 1

Turn to your favorite passage of scripture to preach. Over the next 5 minutes I am asking you to read it as if it were your first time reading it ever. Resist the temptation to see what you have always preached. As you become familiar with the text and not reminisce your sermon points identify a new theme that stands out and a different title you could preach from for a crisis.

Once this is done try to identify at least three possible points of emphasis that will help you make the relevant application to the people. The reason the points are just possibilities is because all of your research has not been done yet. You do not research points you want to preach, but you allow your research to make the points you are going to preach.

Try to get at least three messages that can motivate people during a crisis out of this text. So, do this exercise three times. Do not cheat, you must read the text each time. Once this is done, you should share and discuss what some of your findings were with one of your colleagues for growth and development. This exercise of sharing is called sermonizing. You should always have someone who's preaching preparation and proclamation you admire so you can sermonize before you present to the congregation.

This is done so that you have someone fact check your points of emphasis, as well as your theme and title. They should all have agreement with the text. Or be able to be easily identified in the text that you read.

Homiletics

Homiletics is the study of the composition and delivery of

a sermon or other religious discourse. It includes all forms of preaching, viz., the sermon, homily and catechetical instruction. It may be further defined as the study of the analysis, classification, preparation, composition and delivery of sermons. In short, Homiletics is how we put it together. There is a discipline involved in putting the message in literary form.

We do not simply just get up and preach, but we prepare that which we are going to preach. It is an extension of the science of interpretation. It is the science of preparation. We prepare what we are going to proclaim. We take time to make certain that we are following the disciplines of flow and structure so that what we are saying can be easily comprehended by those who are our listeners. Hermeneutics and *Homiletics* are not caught, but they are taught.

Most do not walk in the door of preaching and teaching simply having an innate ability to rightly divide the word of truth and how to apply it to life. Someone must teach us that. Nor do most of us know how to flawlessly prepare for and construct a public address. Usually, at the very least we must be tutored in this as well.

When we put our presentation together there are several things we must consider immediately.

The subject matter or the text we are preaching or teaching.
Remember we are preaching during a pandemic. It is a crisis. You need to be certain that what you say helps the people manage their very real feelings about the crisis that they are experiencing.

The audience we are addressing.
The audience cannot be understated. Every congregation is a microcosm of the society at large in which the church itself exists. This being the case you must remember that whatever or whomever

you have in your community will be present in your congregation. Good, bad, or ugly, they are there.

Also, you must know the age of your congregation. Do you have a young congregation, or do you have an older congregation? Believe it or not this could change your wording, your points of emphasis and even your style of delivery.

The time we have been allotted.

Time is always of the essence. It is important to not waste the people's time. Make certain that you are on time, the message itself is timely, and you don't take too much time preaching it. A good rule of thumb for preaching is 20-30 minutes. This time should be acceptable wherever you find yourself ministering the word.

The setting or occasion we are attending.

You should be mindful of the venue and program. What you say for a youth revival will definitely be different than what you say on a Sunday morning at one of the most traditional churches in the city. Who's giving the service? Is it the Ushers, the Choir, the Sunday School etc. Who's giving the event could change the development of the message.

When given a subject and a theme always do your best to preach it. At the very least you should acknowledge it. However, bear in mind that sometimes the one who made the theme and found the scripture may not be the best at homiletics, therefore you may have to improvise.

The message we wish to convey.

Dr. Marvin McMickel of Colgate Divinity School use to teach us that we should know the message we want to convey while we are preparing the message. We should know how we want to present the message and how we want the congregation to leave the church after hearing it. Preaching is deliberate.

The result we want to achieve from the presentation.

To that end, do I want the people shouting, thinking, crying, volunteering, changing or angry. The Lord will give us this before we ever show up. He will give us this in the private chambers of our preparation. We then deliver the message accordingly and resist the temptation of allowing the congregation and emotions to carry you to a place that is not your assignment for the day.

As an expositor we have been studying this text, but now we are confronted with what information to use from our studies to make the point of the message clear. We have to search out and through our notes to arrive at a path and direction we must go in to communicate what God has given us to say.

If we watch the preaching of Jesus in scripture his Homiletic approach depended greatly upon His audience, His message, and His location or time. If Jesus were talking to common people oftentimes, He would use parables to expose them to the truth that He was communicating. However, if Jesus were dealing with the academic elite, He would simply argue the theological point at hand. If it were an agrarian culture Jesus would use agrarian terms. If Jesus were dealing with fishermen, He would tell them, "follow me and I will make you fishers of men."

Jesus was a genius at homiletics.

To make this dynamic even simpler I would like to go over with you the ***ABC's of Homiletics.***

A=Accuracy (the information must be both biblical and correct)
B=Brevity (less is more 20-30 minutes)
C=Clarity (communicate clearly so that the youngest in the room can get it)

EXERCISE 2

Using the list of texts that I provided find another text that catches your attention. Take 10 minutes to come up with your own topic and theme. Then try and focus the information in the area you need it to flow in to communicate your points of emphasis or your central theme.

After that is complete take another 5 minutes and develop an introduction for your sermon. Introductions are very important, they set the pace for the preaching or teaching journey. Please remember that introductions can be:

Practical – dealing with everyday events
Historical – dealing with an event in history of the world or country etc.
Textual – dealing with the immediate information of the text
Personal – dealing with a testimony or a personal life experience

Style & Delivery

Believe it or not, this is the part most of us worry about. If the truth be told, all of us want to really deliver a great message. That's okay…I mean who among us wants to suck at presentation???

The key to this section is to not allow the pressure to perform to make you *pretentious*.

Pretentious – expressive of affected, unwarranted, or exaggerated importance, worth, or stature; to make more of something than need be by pretending to be something you are not.

In order for the delivery to be successful the style must be original and sincere. People must feel that we are genuine when we present the Gospel to them. Genuineness is sacrificed when we try to proclaim outside of the gift set that God has given us. It is of the utmost importance that every preacher identifies and recognizes their skill set and gift set and develop what you have to the fullest possible potential of that gift or skill.

As an expositor how do you intend to get the word out?

Will you:

1. *Lecture*
2. *Narrate*
3. *Instruct*
4. *Discuss*
5. *Expound*

There is no "one way" to do it. In fact, you should be skilled in all the ways because you never know what group you may be assigned to. If you are a pastor, it would be good for you to discipline your congregation to be able to receive word in more than just one delivery style.

So many churches believe that if it is not done in a particular fashion then it is not effective. Effectiveness is or should be directly connected to the message that you want to convey. Sometimes it is more important to instruct than it is to celebrate. If my desire is to leave the congregation in deep thought I may not want to whoop.

Several Ways to End a Message
- Motivation
- Contemplation
- Inspiration
- Celebration
- Condemnation

This could change from week to week. Therefore, it is important for us to hear God and not just our egos as we prepare to share the Word of God. The important thing is to make sure that when we present, we are never guilty of having more style than substance or more substance than style. Either combination can make the experience unbearable for those who must listen.

In closing this chapter, please remember that your dress is a part of your presentation. It is absolutely a part of your style and delivery. Therefore, we should always dress appropriately. We should always know where we are going and what is expected. We do not want our appearance to ever be louder than the message we are proclaiming.

Along with this we must remember not to have distracting presence or gestures. Nothing should take the audience's attention off of what is being said.

EXERCISE 3

I want you to determine what style of preacher you desire to be. Don't be shy or ecclesiastical and deep. If you want to whoop and holler and kill the place every week say that. There's nothing wrong with that.

After you declare a style, I want you to make a list of your skills and gifts. Identify what you are exceptional at. Then make a list of things you may not do so well as it relates to proclaiming your message. We have to determine if you have the skill set or gift set to pull off the style you want.

After this is determined we have to decide should you pursue what you initially thought, or should you develop another primary style of preaching that will better showcase your call and your anointing?

Conclusion

I sincerely hope that this chapter has helped you focus in on how you can become a better expository preacher in times of crisis and all the time. I want to share with you a formula for sermon structure that will help you get started disciplining yourself to become an expository preacher. It is the style that my father in the ministry taught me and his father in the ministry taught him and his father in the ministry taught him. It is universal and it will work anywhere.

Step 1 – Introduction
Step 2 – Transitional statement to the text
Step 3 – History of the text

Step 4 – Three points of emphasis
Step 5 – Conclusion
Step 6 – Celebration
Step 7 – Invitation

Use it….it really works!!!

Chapter 8
Knowing the Lord & the Word

It is so easy to get caught up doing the Lord's Work, that we forget, we work for the Lord…without sounding condescending I need to pose a question to consider at the outset of the lesson… Why do you preach???

Whatever preaching, teaching or church is to you is indeed how you will approach it. Before we move forward it is important for you to make sure that preaching means the same thing to you as it does to the Lord. Without this God is not obligated to honor your desire for revelation and proclamation.

Contrary to popular belief there are only two kinds of preaching. There are many styles of preaching, but there are only two kinds of preaching. Literally meaning you can use whatever style you want, the kind of preaching you can do is only twofold.

Please remember that you cannot gauge whether or not you are preaching good by the response of the people. You can only know if you are preaching good by evaluating whether or not your message accomplished your goal for the day. The fact that they shouted is only good if that was your only goal for the day.

Which one you do is determined by three things: *Preparation, Structure and Delivery or Presentation.*

Without putting in the work and the time to get all of the previously mentioned points you will be trying to write from a very skewed and fragmented revelation. You will only have clear vision into the text on what you disciplined yourself to be exposed to. Whatever you have not exposed yourself to leaves you with fragments.

If we can only know in part, how much worse is it to now must serve fragments because you didn't take time to get the whole part???

We must learn how to appreciate the different vantage points of each text. The different Vantage Points simply gives us a clear context. It is very important to know the context before you try to interpret the text. Text is what is written, context is why it was written and how it was written. You can only interpret the text properly if you have proper context. Greek and Hebrew means nothing without context.

Ministry can be very thankless work. It can be the norm to serve and serve with faithfulness yet never hear anyone celebrate your efforts or your consistency. This type of ministerial atmosphere can cause the man or woman of God to experience burnout in large numbers. This usually occurs because we are looking for confirmation instead of consecration.

Confirmation means to give approval
: to **ratify** *confirm* a treaty
: to make firm or firmer : **strengthen** *confirm* one's resolve
: to administer the rite of **confirmation** to
: to give new assurance of the validity of : remove doubt about by authoritative act or indisputable fact *confirm* a rumor *confirm* an order dedicated to a sacred purpose...

We spend so much time waiting on people to vouch for us that we miss out on the privilege of God setting us apart. As we wait for people to say we are okay we are missing meaningful opportunities to simply be what God has already sanctioned and called us to be.

We have been saddled with timidity and uncertainty because we have been made to believe that we can only "be" if someone gives us permission to be. It is not up to pastors and bishops and overseers to make you who you are. It is up to you to be who you are, and God will give them discernment to see you.

Your shepherd/leader is only allowed to see you and acknowledge you. He or she cannot give you favor. Favor must come from God if it is favor at all. We are trying to impress flesh as opposed to serving faithfully and it will leave us feeling empty and unappreciated. However, speaking as a pastor of more than thirty years…It's hard for me to discern your gift in all of the deafening desperation of your ego.

I need you to settle down and serve so I can see what God gave you as opposed to you endlessly talking about what you feel you can do and should be doing. In short…this is service.

I need to say here that if you struggle with this, this is not your fault. This fault belongs squarely to the leadership of churches everywhere because we have allowed the systems and practices of the world and corporate America to slip into the church. So, we function in the church like we do in the world. I am on assignment to make certain that you function the way God intended you to function.

Fine Tuning Functionality

Believe God Called Me

You cannot and must not wait to have your calling validated by other people. The call to ministry is both powerful and real. The key to authentication is owning what type of call you received and embracing it.

Everyone who has a calling of God does not hear the voice of God aloud or even in their head. There are those who testify that they literally heard God call them and I believe them. I believe what they say their experience was. This is called a primary call. That means they heard God directly call them into ministry. This is not just possible, but it's biblical. This is how Samuel, Isaiah and Jeremiah all received their calls.

However, there is another group who did not receive their call in this way. They had a *secondary call* experience. That means God did not call them audibly. They did not hear a heavenly voice commission them into the service of the Lord. They received their call from a leader in church that they trust emphatically.

Someone in their life or, in ministry that they respect, love and trust came to them and told them that they had a vision, or heard a word from the Lord concerning them and that they are supposed to preach. This type of call is not just okay, it is also biblical.

Then finally, there is the call that I call the *tertiary call*. In this experience someone committed to God decides that they want to preach, and others affirm the decision. This call is frowned upon by so many, but I ask the question, what's wrong with wanting to preach and doing it, if you're going to commit your life to doing it.

Let's face it, there are many with fantastic call stories that are blasphemous at best as it relates to their ministerial conduct and commitment. Why not choose God and be committed to Him? I have no problem with the one who receives their call in this fashion and I openly support them, and would rather train them then someone who refuses to honor the cleric's call.

Believe God has Equipped Me (specifically)

I must believe that God has equipped me to do what He has called me to do. The quickest way to doubt this is through comparisons. Please do not compare the way you do it with anyone else. God has uniquely called you. He knows what your gift set is already. You already have everything you need to be a great tool in the hands of our awesome God. Resist the temptation to imitate others. Be you and watch God use you.

Believe My Primary Objective is to Serve

We are all servants. If you were to go to a fancy restaurant and ask for the manager because your server was not that good. When the manager comes yes, he has a different title, yes, he has a different dress code, but at the end of the day the manager is still a servant.

We may have different titles: Bishop, Apostle, Pastor, Elder, Minister, Prophet etc. Please remember at the end of the day, your garments may be different, the color of your cord might be different, but we are all servants.

Believe Preparation Produces Performance

Be the preacher that the people came to hear. Never be the preacher that the people will tolerate. When you prepare yourself, you will become the preference in the room. Because great preparation will always maximize your performance.

Believe God Desires Humility & Boldness

Let the Lord be your agent. Let God promote you. Let God open doors for you. You promote this Great Gospel. You serve as a humble servant and God will never let your well of opportunities run dry.

If you do it the other way where you are constantly pushing your way through and making room for yourself, I promise you, your life will be a series of dry seasons.

Believe Gift & Office are Totally Different

My office and my gift are totally separate. The gift is what I possess the office is what possesses me. I must be certain not to become my position, but just serve effectively in them as they come to me.

Believe I am Necessary & Needed

If I were not, God would have never created me.

I am a movie buff. I love the movies. In every movie there are people in the movie who have no real role. These people are called stand ins. The stand ins are there to fill in empty spaces. They make things look realistic, but they have no real role in the production. I am happy to report, God does not use stand ins. Every single person He created has a part to play. You are not just here taking up space.

Let Him Use You...

Who Needs Me???
> God Needs Me...
> My Family Needs Me...
> My Church Needs Me...
> My Community Needs Me...

*They need me to be the best version of me that I can both offer and sacrifice.

The Changing of the Guard

In case we haven't noticed, the pastorate has changed forever. Being a senior pastor of a church does not mean what it meant just 20 short years ago. This has not happened because the devil is busy. This has not happened simply because times are changing. I believe this has happened as a strategic plan of our God.

In the last decade research has come out that is clearly informing us of two things:

1. Pastors are quitting at an alarming rate
2. The Church of Jesus Christ in America is shrinking.

   1700 pastors leave ministry every month

Reasons for Running…

- 90% of pastors report working between 55 to 75 hours per week and 50% feel unable to meet the demands of the job.
- And 70% of pastors feel grossly underpaid.
- Most pastors feel unprepared.
- 90% feel they are inadequately trained to cope with the ministry demands and 90% of pastors said the ministry was completely different than what they thought it would be like before they entered the ministry.
- Many pastors struggle with depression and discouragement.
- 70% of pastors constantly fight depression and 50% of pastors feel so discouraged that they would leave the ministry if they could but have no other way of making a living.
- 80% believe pastoral ministry has negatively affected their families. 80% of spouses feel the pastor is overworked and feel left out and under-appreciated by church members.

This Lack of Leadership Causes Shrinkage...

We tend to localize the Matthew 16:18 text and apply the language to our churches, but to the contrary the text is about the Universal Body of Christ. It is about the Kingdom.

The Church of Jesus Christ is indeed expanding all over the globe. However, in America it is shrinking. Here are some statistics that I would like to share with you so that we might center our dialogue on why fearless Pastors are needed so desperately in this day and age.

The US Department of State estimates that Protestant Christianity may have grown 600% over the last decade in Vietnam.

Africa

Christianity has been estimated to be growing rapidly in South America, Africa, and Asia. In Africa, for instance, in 1900, there were only 8.7 million adherents of Christianity; now there are 390 million, and it is expected by 2025 there will be 600 million Christians in Africa.

In America, 3500-4000 churches close their doors each year. *(from the Barna Study, www.barna.org)*

› Churches lose an estimated 2,765,000 people each year to nominalism and secularism. *(from the Barna Study, www.barna.org)*
› Usual Sunday church attendance has from dropped from 1,606,00 in 1968 to 881,000 in 2005. *(www.churchsociety.org)*

America

Each year 3,500 to 4,000 churches close their doors forever; yet only 1,100 to 1,500 new churches are started.

Even though America has more people, it has fewer churches per capita than at any time in her history. Although the number of churches in America has increased by 50 percent in the last century, the new churches adopt new methods and adapt new strategies for reaching people and ministering to them more effectively than existing churches.

> *"There exists a flawed understanding that the United States and Canada are already evangelized. While there is abundant access to Christian information, many unchurched persons in North America are amazingly untouched by the evangelical subculture because the Christian subculture is largely incapable of providing a culturally relevant gospel witness."* –Ed Stezer

One of the things we readily perpetuate concerning preaching is that somehow presentation does not really matter. We often say that as long as we get up and share from our heart the truth that everything will be alright. My assertion for today is nothing could be further from the truth!!!

For my presentation to be polished, my heart must change. I cannot preach from a premise of me, I must preach from a premise of Him. Therefore, the origin of my sermonic thoughts must match his word and his will for me and the people to which I am preaching. I am always a part of the congregation, not apart from the congregation.

It is a rare occasion for God to send us to a people to which we have nothing in common. When God does this, He is doing so to keep the message pure as in the case of Joseph or Amos. Usually, the preacher or prophet has a connection with the audience he or she is addressing…and it is not always a positive trait.

With specificity there is a reason why God has given us the assignment for the day. God literally has millions of preachers. For any of us to have an assignment on any given day is a miracle of biblical proportions. So, why has He chosen you for the day? In what way should the people leave your sermonic experience? Remember these from the previous chapter.

Praise

God has been good to us. There are times when God wants his people to simply praise him. He wants them to become undone. He wants them suspended from every problem they could consider and just praise Him in spirit and in truth. While this can't be every Sunday, we should bask in the Sundays He allows us to be totally uninhibited in his presence.

Contemplation

There are times when the Lord does not want the people to leave shouting and undone in emotion. There are times when the Lord wants us to leave thinking. He wants us in deep contemplative thought about forgiveness, or ministry, or that person on our job who we may have an issue with, or our families.

Conviction

There are times when the Lord wants us to be ashamed of ourselves. He wants the message to take the people to the place of confession and repentance. He wants the congregation leaving with doing better for Him on their minds.

Deliverance

God has always been and forever will be a deliverer. There are some services where the message and the altar appeal both need to be conducive for deliverance. We need to prepare ourselves to do less preaching on these days and more ministering by way of prayer and laying on of hands.

Commissioned

God can want the preacher to preach a message that commissions the entire congregation to do something. It's not just a sermon, it is a strategical planning session, and the people are ready work.

Challenged

Sometimes a challenge must be given so the people can become their best selves. Though sobering, this is a very powerful way to leave a congregation.

Salvation/Rededication

This is it!!! There is nothing greater than a soul being saved, or a prodigal coming home. This result at the altar will create its own celebration. The saints still love to see people saved and set free.

Whatever the assignment is for the day please accept it and remember that power does not come while we preach or as we preach. The power of God comes and rests upon us before we preach. Without this you will be all style with no substantive presence. There is a place where God meets us before we ever stand up. It's important to have this meeting lest we waste the people's time.

"Preaching is most powerful when you show up as you, being used by him…." –Bishop Kenneth Wayne Paramore, D. Min.

Chapter 9
Conclusion

I pray this project has helped you. I pray that the time you spent reading this was not a waste of time, but that it has inspired you to be the best version of yourself for the One, True and Living God.

I want you to know that while this book is entitled *"Pandemic Preaching,"* the tools I shared with you and the truth that was imparted is useful no matter where you may find yourself in this ministerial journey. But please remember the people need to hear from us the most, not when everything is going the way they want it, but when their backs are against the wall and they are petrified about what's coming up next.

I need for you to stop shrinking in those moments and be the preacher/leader God has called you to be.

This pandemic has been something else. I have never seen anything like it in my 54 years of life. Yet, I believe God and I believe the Word of God. I believe that all of these things are happening for a profound supernatural reason. I am speaking of everything from the pandemic, to the racial and social injustices, right down to this crazy presidential election. I believe that God is doing something.

In closing this project, I would like to share with you what I believe it is.

I believe that the church has been very negligent in so many areas. Preaching, teaching, training, and so many others. I believe our greatest sin has been in how we have handled the LGBTQ community and those who struggle with addictions. I believe that we have ostracized both of these groups in a profoundly unforgettable way.

The hate speech and the indifference has been nothing short of evil and I believe in this list of things mentioned is how we lost our power and influence in our country.

I am praying and asking God to forgive us for our negligence in love and the word. And I am asking God to restore unto us the Joy of our salvation and to return our supernatural power for "Great Works" once again. I am certain that this will not come to us all, because I believe the word. But I do believe that there is a remnant who will do it the Lord's way.

My request is for you to join and be a part of the remnant. God still has greater works for us to do in his Kingdom.

Bless You

About the Author

Bishop Paramore is an anointed man of God. He was born, reared and educated in Youngstown, Ohio. He pursued his education further by relocating to Akron, Ohio where he received a Bachelor's Degree from the University of Akron, his Master's Degree from Ashland Theological Seminary and his Doctorate of Ministry from United Theological Seminary.

While in Akron, Ohio he answered the call into ministry that he had received earlier in life. Fellowshipping with United Baptist Church, he would be taught and learn the ministry. God blessed him and opened up numerous doors to be used. He served his first pastorate at Shiloh Missionary Baptist Church, Akron, Ohio. God would later call him back to United Baptist Church, to serve as pastor.

While in revival in Chicago, Illinois, God spoke to him through a prophetic word, that he would be used in ministry in his native home of Youngstown, Ohio. He would immediately begin to plan and prepare for what God was going to do. Upon hearing from God, he opened the Christian Revival and Discipleship Center. It started as a weekly bible study. The purpose was to rekindle the fire of the saints, who were disgruntled with the church and the people of God. Once they were revived, then they would be ready to be a disciple and ready to work for the Lord. Under the guidance and direction of the Lord, this weekly bible study would develop into a church. God would speak again and ordain for CRDC to open in Canton, Ohio, which has now relocated to Barberton, Ohio. Pastor Paramore was blessed to serve at United and CRDC. After serving at United for 15 years God released him and has blessed him to continue the ministry of CRDC.

While attending a leadership conference in Alabama, God would speak again through a prophetic word. He prayed and God led him to change the name to The Christ Centered Church. While continuing to follow God, Bishop Paramore is currently leading and directing Christ Centered Church.

Bishop Paramore is the founder of Bradley Bible College. This is an accredited bible college that is named after one of his mentors Dr. I. T. Bradley. It is currently housed in Youngstown, Barberton and Mansfield, Ohio.

In June of 2013, Bishop Paramore began fellowshipping with Kingdom Connection Fellowship International. He was consecrated to the office of Bishop in June of 2014. He currently serves his apostolic father Bishop Jerome H. Ross Sr. by training the pastors, ministers and elders in KCFI. Bishop Paramore was released from his official assignment as the Bishop of the College of Ministers and Elders to initiate a reformation for this present age. LIFTED Reformation of Christian Churches of which he co-founded with several of his ministerial colleagues.

A great milestone was reached in his life as he is now a published author. *She Cost Too Much* is his first book that was released in September of 2015. *Single Minded* was released in August of 2018.

Bishop Paramore is married and the father of three children.

www.ingramcontent.com/pod-product-compliance
Lightning Source LLC
Chambersburg PA
CBHW071155090426
42736CB00012B/2342